I Am The Mother of Sons

Poems by Jayne Jaudon Ferrer

Illustrated by Lina Levy

POCKET BOOKS

New York • London • Toronto • Sydney • Tokyo • Singapore

POCKET BOOKS, a division of Simon & Schuster Inc.
1230 Avenue of the Americas, New York, NY 10020

Copyright © 1996 by Jayne Jaudon Ferrer

ISBN: 0-671-52435-6

First Pocket Books hardcover printing May 1996

10 9 8 7 6 5 4 3 2 1

POCKET and colophon are registered trademarks of
Simon & Schuster Inc.

Book design by Patrice Kaplan and Gina Bonanno

Printed in Mexico

For Jaron, James, and John—
with all my love,
till the last day.

Acknowledgments

After the birth of my first son, I wrote a collection of poetry entitled *A New Mother's Thoughts*. It was gentle, and sweet, and made women cry. Then I had another son. And another. And I knew it was time to create another collection.

This book isn't gentle and sweet, but you still might cry—with relief—because those of us who mother sons share a special bond of agony and ecstasy. (Do mothers of girls get love offerings of caterpillars and frogs?) Sons require a unique blend of patience, energy, and pride; in return, they offer unfailing enthusiasm, unlimited loyalty, and lifelong love (hold the kisses).

It's harder to find time for writing these days, because life in a houseful of boys tends to shove aside contemplative moments. I am grateful, therefore, to my friend Susan Kleto for jump-starting my languishing muse at a critical moment. I would also like to thank the following: Jane

Comer and Joyce Bethea for constant support, encouragement, and prayers; Miss Jean, Miss Billie Jean, and Miss Carole for appreciating my sons'…um…*zest* for life; my sister Vera, for reading and weeping; my husband, Jose, for tolerating my weird hours and condoning a passion he doesn't always like or understand; my son John, who is now old enough to know he's being talked about and loves me anyway; my son James, whose grin keeps me going on the toughest days; my son Jaron, whose kisses make getting up worth it after writing half the night; my agent, Meg Ruley, who has, for years now, offered advice, dispensed direction, and negotiated deals as if I were her most valuable author; my editorial team, whose attention and interest to this little book is tremendously rewarding; and my publisher, who decided my words were a worthwhile investment—twice!

$\mathcal{I}$ am a woman blessed with many things; a quiet household is not one of them. May you find solace and satisfaction in these pages.

Jayne Jaudon Ferrer

Trueborn Times

*Boys are much better than girls, 'cause they can fight,
and be ninjas, and dance cool, and burp.*
—James, age five

As Gallagher Says, We're Different

There is no pink in my house.
Just a rough-ridged rainbow of
red, yellow, and blue
as Legos
(and guns—not real ones, not even toy ones,
just imaginary ones that began life
as azalea twigs and shoe horns)
coagulate in my carpet
and propagate
like alley cat kudzu.
Battle cries.
War whoops.
Raucous laughter.
Loud burps.
Silence, if it comes, sits

only long enough for grace.
Even then, testosterone rears its rowdy head:
Me do it!
No, *Me!!*
No, Me!!!
Thanks get returned in triplicate
at 80 decibels and 90 miles an hour
as each one tries to make sure
his words get to God
first.

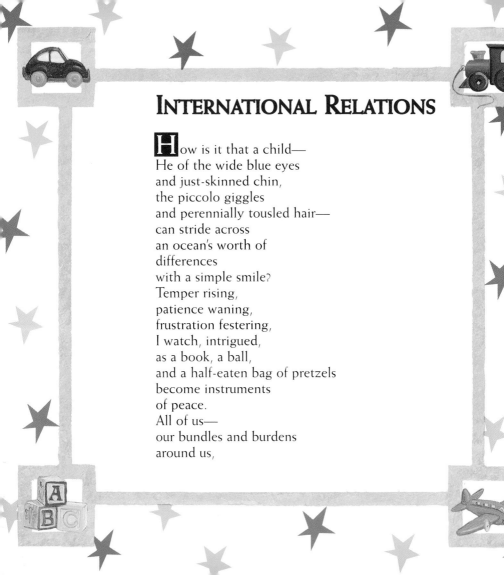

INTERNATIONAL RELATIONS

How is it that a child—
He of the wide blue eyes
and just-skinned chin,
the piccolo giggles
and perennially tousled hair—
can stride across
an ocean's worth of
differences
with a simple smile?
Temper rising,
patience waning,
frustration festering,
I watch, intrigued,
as a book, a ball,
and a half-eaten bag of pretzels
become instruments
of peace.
All of us—
our bundles and burdens
around us,

our tension and tightness
inside us—
become happenstance voyeurs.
Prisoners of the moment,
our lives put on hold
by conditions not conducive
to flight.
We sit dully in the terminal,
sheep without a shepherd,
too…stupid? sleepy? stiff? to make the most
of the moment.
But this!
This boy-child I have born,
pent-up preschool power
fairly crackling in the
bored, dry air,
yanks fate's faux pas
into his own pudgy fingers.
Tired of TV,
disenchanted with assorted grandma-types and me,
he spots a fellow traveler across the way.

Nonplussed by dark hair,
darker eyes, and bejeweled skin,
he holds out his treasures:
"Wanna share?"
She, stunned and shy,
retreats, but smiles.
He, in a gesture that would
make Miss Scarlett swoon,
addresses her mama:
"It's okay, I'm a nice boy,
and I will just give her some
pretzels, okay? Because
we're *hungry!* "
So they share a snack
without sharing a language,
forge a friendship without
formulating an agreement,
revel in the fact that
they're both four
and fun to be with
and the rest just
doesn't much matter.
We all learned a little bit
that day.

ATTACK OF THE DIAPERED VIKING

I hear it once again.
The staccato breaths,
impatient pants,
and pawing palms.
Then finally comes
the valiant growl
of conquest—
"Aiiiiiiiiiiiihhhh!"—
and I watch bemused as
once again you plunge forth
in unflinching pursuit
of the notorious lamp cord.
Fair skin, fiery curls,
and full diaper firmly in place,
you look like Erik the Red
come to vanquish a port.
Is this the spirit with which
you'll go forth
to conquer the world?
If it is, dear boy,
the battle's already fought;
the victory yours!

PERSPECTIVE

My heart breaks when I hear the words:
"Mommy, am I bad?"
O, vile tongue!
You who have mocked this child
with your sarcasm,
screamed at his pint-sized destruction,
threatened his very existence!
O, hateful hand!
You who have shaken in anger
that head of bright curls,
slapped outstretched arms
that refused to withdraw,
pointed the way to recluse
down the hall.

O, wounded heart!
This, my challenge child,
the one who
daily
takes me to the edge of tolerance
then yanks me back
into a canyon of love,
who engineers feats
of abject desecration beyond
my wildest conjuring,
while oozing preciousness
and precociousness
and plain old irresistible
spunk
from every sweet, sweaty
little boy pore.
No, my darling,
you are not bad.
You are overwhelmingly
wonderful.

COWBOY COOKIES

It was on the way to Grandma's,
I think.
Entrepreneurial embers flaming,
desperate for something to do
besides count birds or
listen to (God forbid) Barney again,
you actually worked together
       peacefully
         —even pleasantly!—
and "Cowboy Cookies" were born.
Casing the billboards on I-75,
you concurred competition was tough.
But what kid could resist, you reasoned,
cowboys and horses and hats
served up in three favorite flavors?
By the time we got there,
you'd gone from cookies to complete cuisine:
"PowWow Pancakes," "Hiawatha Hot Dogs,"
"Cone Rangers" and "Silver Sundaes"…
You guys still laugh and recall that trip
once in a while;
the memory is still
delicious
after all these years.

WORD PICTURES

Denim and boots,
white Sunday suits,
kisses and giggles,
wet beds and wiggles,
monsters and fables,
climbing on tables,
baseballs and bats,
pulled tails of cats,
crayons and mud,
bruises and blood,
guns, forts, and sticks,
voilá! magic tricks,
video games,
hot cars and airplanes,
back talk and bragging,
car keys and nagging,
acne and hair creams,
night jobs and daydreams,
tuition and classes,
mascaraed lashes,
résumés, rings,
taxes, rent, grown-up things…
My little boy's gone;
how time marches on!

Tender
Times

Mom, I love you sixty-seven fifty. Is that a lot?
—Jaron, age four

MIDNIGHT RENDEZVOUS

It is with something less than
maternal goodwill that I crawl,
asleep and annoyed, from my
coveted bed to
silence your angry screams
violating the night.
We rock in the chair
that has been ours since
the very beginning,
ensconced in Great-Grandmother's
crocheted afghan and a
ghostly green light
from the VCR.
Mute now, but for pitiful,
periodic whimpers, you
cling to me like some
abandoned creature reclaimed.

Clinging back,
I am EveryMother, an
all-knowing, all-loving,
all-bestowing, all-forgiving
paragon of matriarchal perfection.
Feeling your sweet, soundless
breaths tease the tangled hair
on the back of my neck,
the last trace of irritation over
interrupted sleep swiftly
dissipates in a hug, a kiss,
and a smile.
You will never remember
these tender midnight moments
together;
I will never forget. ☻

MOTHERLODE

Like porpoises frolicking on
a perfect, sunstreaked day,
or fat puppies practicing
fun, but unfamiliar, parts,
we squeal and growl and
clutch and collide in time
to no one's rhythm
but our own.
Shrieking, you fall on my face
openmouthed
with ardor and wet kisses
no college boy could ever hope
to top.

Giggling, I seize five
of those twenty, tiny, tireless
tips/toes, the ones which
never seem to still themselves
for an instant, then
consume them, piece by piece,
in savoring chomps.
How marvelous to explore
the wonder of each other,
unencumbered by consequence
or clocks!
We are two in a private
universe of discovery,
each new find
a treasure chest
to fund tomorrow's adventures. ☻

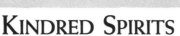

KINDRED SPIRITS

You, eldest son,
with the face of your father,
the grin of your granddad,
are mine.

In your eyes that look
like his,
I see myself—
searching for secrets,
summoning truth,
offering acceptance
in a warm gray gaze.

Spirit clones, we—
fueled by images
     and words
     and wonderment
long after others
have bid day adieu.

The world is different
in those onyx hours:
silent…serene…uncensored…
the time when our souls speak the loudest;
the time when our hearts hear best.

CARPE DIEM

Y ou, middle child of mine—
whose heart do *you* have?
(Mine, of course;
you stole it years ago.)
But whose *are* you?
Affectionate, quick-witted,
imbued with incessant joie de vivre…
you stand, stalwart, with arms open wide,
welcoming each moment of life
like a long-lost friend.
I envy your aplomb—
applaud it—
and ponder which ancestor's
congenial gene pool
deserves credit for your
energy level. ✹

EARTH ANGEL

You, my youngest one—
lover of music,
champion of animals,
jubilant nightsprite that never sleeps,
I long to know what lies ahead for you.

Feisty, yet fragile,
intent on achieving, come what may,
you trudge on
long after the rest of us fade or
fall dormant.
That twinkle in your eye,
that twitch in your dashing dimple—
are they part of the magic that makes you
so bold and invincible?

I know!
You are an angel,
bequeathed to earth
when heaven's fair host
could no longer sustain you. ✪

COMMAND PERFORMANCE

It's when he sings to me
I ache for time to stop.
Just-cut blond bangs
framing a face so pure
it is that of heaven,
the notes come softly—
giggle-laced and laden
with pride
as familiar tunes
meander valiantly
through still-awkward syllables.
While the older ones
roll eyes in bored disgust,
I am rapt,
on fire with love,
tears a mere pulse away from my smile
as
            frenzied
my heart records every image
from eyelash to hiccup
for replays on Memory Lane
when this show closes
to make way for the next.

Tumultuous Times

"Son, I don't like to see you swinging that shovel."
"Well, close your eyes, Dad!"
—Sam, age three

Morning Reverie

Oh, great.
It's 7:30.
I don't know; I'm in the bathroom.
Fix your lunch.
Did you finish your homework?
I don't *know;* I'm in the *bathroom.*
What do you *mean* you don't have any
clean underwear?!
Oh, great, no tampons.
Parachutes for the seven dwarfs??
What were…never mind.
I don't know!!! I'll be out in a minute!!!
You *have* to eat Pop-Tarts; we're late.
It's due *today???*
Would the dwarfs have needed my *panty hose,*
by any chance?

Turn off that television!
Clean up that mess!
You can't wear that.
Don't call your brother names.
I don't know! I don't wear them!!!
Somebody get the dog out of the house.
You're *still* not dressed???
Oh, great, who left the gas tank empty?
Shut the door!
Turn the radio down.
Stop hitting your brother!
Put that seat belt on!
Could you all shut *up?!* You're driving me crazy!!
Well, what do you know, we got here before
second period...
Okay, bye, babes, have a nice day,
love ya!! 🧸

THE BEST INTENTIONS

I don't believe in treating
all children alike.
So I bought one
dinosaur place mat,
one alphabet place mat,
and one
with a map of the world.
I've decided
children shouldn't have place mats.
And if they do,
they should all be
plain white.

THE BOYS CLUB

We know who we are.
Ours is like one of those ancient, fraternal orders
whose identifying rituals
include elaborate hand signals and
mysterious primal grunts.
In McDonald's, of course,
the cue tends to be
a series of short, repetitive barks:

> "Sit *down!*"
> "*Give* me that!"
> "Come *here!*"
> "*Now!*"

People who aren't in the club
look disdainful, or annoyed,
or disgusted, or smug.
But fellow members grin.
Slowly, at first, as they
identify and empathize…
then broadly, as they catch your eye
and nod slightly to acknowledge
familiar phrases
and well-known responses.
"Boys are somethin', ain't they?!"

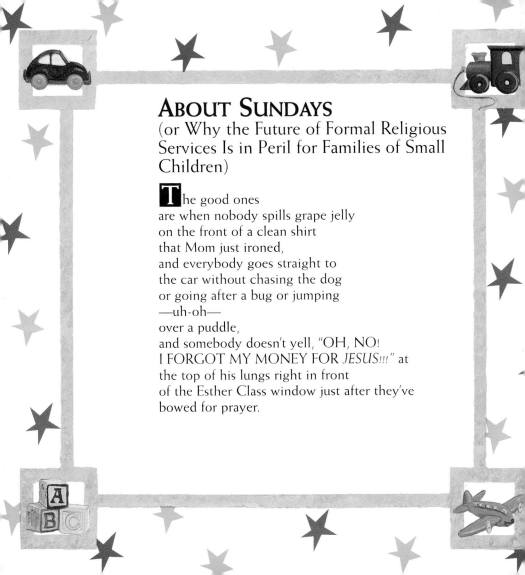

ABOUT SUNDAYS
(or Why the Future of Formal Religious
Services Is in Peril for Families of Small
Children)

The good ones
are when nobody spills grape jelly
on the front of a clean shirt
that Mom just ironed,
and everybody goes straight to
the car without chasing the dog
or going after a bug or jumping
—uh-oh—
over a puddle,
and somebody doesn't yell, "OH, NO!
I FORGOT MY MONEY FOR *JESUS!!!*" at
the top of his lungs right in front
of the Esther Class window just after they've
bowed for prayer.

The bad ones
are when somebody thinks the
preacher's rhetorical questions
require earnest, honest, clearly enunciated answers,
and everybody waves at
Dad in the choir loft, and
in sign language loud enough to reach
Borneo, points out their own
exemplary behavior, and the very
rude antics of their siblings,
and nobody has a clue
why Mom feels a
headache coming on
every Saturday night.

A DAY IN THE LIFE

He *hit* me!
He *pushed* me!
I had that ball first!
That airplane is *mine!*
Mom, make him *stop!*
I'm *telling!*
You *jerk-head!*
He won't *share!*
It's *my* turn!
Mom, he's not being *fair!*
He said a *bad* word!
I *don't* have to!
He's messing *everything* up!
You're gonna be in trouble!
Mom, come here!
I *mean* it!
You're *stupid!*
Can, *too!*
I'm not *playing* with you anymore!

I'm bored.
This is no fun.
Can we come out now?
We'll play outside.
We promise.
Thanks, Mom!

You *hit* me!
You *pushed* me!
I had that toy first!
That stick is *mine!*
Mom, make him *stop!*
I'm *telling!*
You *jerk-head!*

. . .

LESSON REVIEW

Have I taught you the right things,
my darlings?
In between laundry and table-setting,
ironing and pants-hemming,
manners
and morals
and where to pin the corsage,
did I remember to teach about love?
About listening and hearing
and holding and helping
and *always* remembering to put the toilet seat down?

While I ferried you to lessons and
parties and games,
did I find time to talk about life?
About philosophy and philanthropy
and ethics and art
and *never* to leave before the credits have run?

There's so much!
You must know about
politics, heretics,
deferment, fulfillment,
pain, civic duty,
civil rights, inner beauty…

Oh, I wanted to teach you *everything*, darlings!
        But life is so brief
        and its wonders so vast.
There's no textbook for teaching
Life, Or How to Turn Boys into Men.
So please—
just keep asking me what's on the test.

Treasured Times

Hasn't this been just the bestest day?
—John, age three

ALMANAC

It is summer.
I know from
wild, primal whoops
that echo clear in the grass-tinged
afternoon stillness.
From
firm-fleshed rumps glistening
like peaches in the breeze
as one, two, *three!*
they bounce in
front yard sprinklers and
backyard pools.
I know from
sweat-damp foreheads
and blackberry-moist chins,
chubby hands clenched
around ice-picked pickle jars
blinking twi-light
              twi-light
                     twi-i-i-i-light
in the cabernet softness.

It is fall.
I know from
dancing eyes and
cinnamon cheeks
that peek over smiling wisps
of cocoa.
From
cowboy boots scuffling
boisterously
through restless topaz and crimson leaves
like tiny torpedoes
streaking into a school of
skittish guppies.
I know from
pumpkins,
their smooth flesh
hacked and jagged
where virgin fingers sought to
create ghouls
from a simple gourd.

It is winter.
I know from
giddy whispers
in the halls,
carillon giggles
that rival cherished carols
in their sweet, simple
melodies of joy.
From
fingertips frosted
pink as a newborn kitten's nose,
their woolly red cocoons flung aside
in pursuit of the perfect snowball.
I know from
footsteps
in the final chill
of dawn's descent,
a prelude
to softly rooting heads and
feebly flailing limbs
in search of warmth
and safe haven
for a few moments more.

It is spring.
I know from
sweaters slung
impatiently
around slim denim hips,
the sole concession made
to still-brisk mornings.
From lace—Queen Anne's—
pieceworked with just-plucked stems
of milkweed and Lazy Susans
presented in a pride-filled fist.
I know from
bunnies,
chocolate ones and
fuzzy ones and
terrified ones
clutched in smudged,
mercurachromed arms
I hope will always
make room
for me.

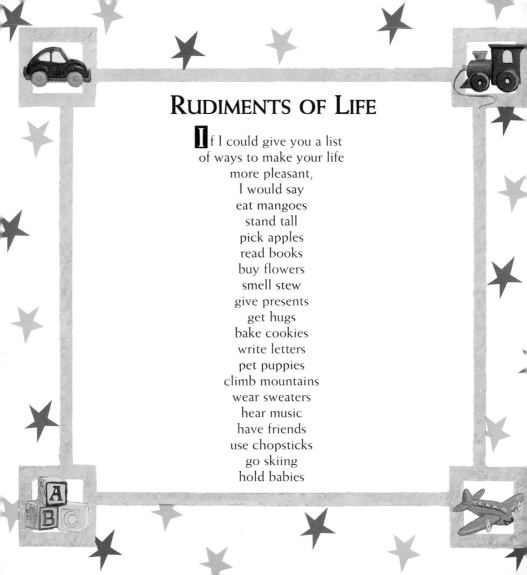

RUDIMENTS OF LIFE

If I could give you a list
of ways to make your life
more pleasant,
I would say
eat mangoes
stand tall
pick apples
read books
buy flowers
smell stew
give presents
get hugs
bake cookies
write letters
pet puppies
climb mountains
wear sweaters
hear music
have friends
use chopsticks
go skiing
hold babies

fly kites
watch clouds
sing often
breathe deeply
attend church
avoid politics
acquire patience
ignore idiots
pray daily
cry often
smile slowly
laugh heartily
be truthful
share knowledge
ask questions
spread blankets
plan picnics
kiss gently
say thank you
save keepsakes
celebrate regularly
love lots.

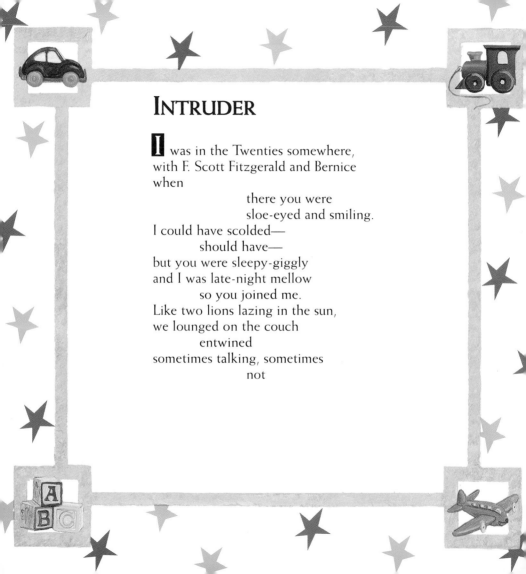

INTRUDER

I was in the Twenties somewhere,
with F. Scott Fitzgerald and Bernice
when

there you were
sloe-eyed and smiling.
I could have scolded—
should have—
but you were sleepy-giggly
and I was late-night mellow
so you joined me.
Like two lions lazing in the sun,
we lounged on the couch
entwined
sometimes talking, sometimes
not

about little things
and life things
and nothings.
And some time in the night,
after popcorn
            and Hershey bars
            and water
            and lots of wiggling
            and a couple of trips to the bathroom
you fell asleep
and I fell in love
            all over again.

SWING TIME

Here we go, looby-loo,
Here we go, looby-lie
Here I go pushing you,
All the way up to the sky.

Watching you swing
is my favorite thing.
Pure joy,
reckless abandon.
Reaching for heaven,
gliding to earth.
Swinging days
are special days
dipped in fragrance of grass,
caressed with tip-toe breezes,
languidly french-kissed
by the sun.
Days
filled with the music of
your laughter, my love,
and the insouciant (indignant?) repertoire
of the mockingbird
just above.

REQUIEM, FOR MY SONS

If I died tomorrow,
contented I would go.
For in my time on earth
I've had the chance
to get to know your hearts,
your minds, your spirits…
and, oh! what bliss it's been!
to watch the world through
your eyes, see you learning
to be men.
You've shown me courage,
laughter, passion, anguish,
pride;
dreams, curiosity, wisdom—
Life, personified.
And though I'd long to know down
which path each of you will stray,
I'd take great joy in having gone along
part of the way. ▲

Temporal Times

🚲
---

*When I grow up, I'm going to be an Air Force pilot
and my wife will probably work at the exchange or own
an art shop, and have black hair, and I'll have three kids
and name them Cruiser, Enus, and Toots, or Cruiser,
Maverick, and Turbo.*
—Sam, age nine

I AM THE MOTHER OF SONS

I am the mother of sons—
robust boys with curly hair
and sunburst smiles
and a penchant for ice cream
and frogs.

I am the mother of sons—
pale boys with velvet eyes
and contemplative souls
and not enough time
to do nothing.

I am the mother of sons—
dark boys with gentle hearts
and troubled minds
and spirits that sprint back
inexplicably.

I am the mother of sons—
frail babes with frantic cries
and feeble grips
who dare not imagine
tomorrow.

I am the mother of sons—
proud boys with shoulders squared
who, nobly, stood for
democracy's sake,
fell heroes on foreign soil.

I am the mother of sons—
humble men whose blood
purged the souls of all sons,
whose love will engulf us
forever.

EVIL IS ITS NAME

It's bound to happen.
No matter how hard
you hide the headlines,
shush up the six o'clock news,
and recite the rhyme about sticks and stones,
sooner or later
hatred and prejudice assault them.
Would that the bad guys always wore black hats,
so categorically,
like the shepherd dividing the sheep and the
goats,
you could say these people
are good, and
these people
are bad.
But ignorance isn't marked with a Stetson.
And sadly, the vilest epithets they hear
may come from some
they love.

There's Deacon Joe, who preaches love
but solicits Boy Scouts by surname…
Great-aunt Sara, whose ethnic jokes
are a highlight at the weekly bridge club…
Mrs. Willis, who bakes cakes for every family
in the neighborhood except the one
she terms "not our kind."
How in the world do you
ever explain Anne Frank,
pro-lifers who kill,
Sarajevo,
bad cops,
or the four-year-old who got shot
through his window
while eating Spaghettios
last night?
You don't.
You just keep planting flowers
and hope
they choke out
the despicable weeds.

INQUIRING HEARTS

Ah, women.
He wants me to explain them.
Young, blond ones,
in particular.
Well, I'm blond,
and I was young…
but how do I tell him
she'll break his heart?
How do I say
"Be careful!"
without sounding like, well,
a mother?

How do I let him know
that there will be many
more blondes—
and likely a brunette or two, too—
before THE ONE
lays claim to his heart
for good?
Somehow, I think
all he really wants me
to explain
is how to gracefully ask
Girl #2 to the dance
if Miss Girl of His Dreams
turns him down. ♫

IMAGE IS EVERYTHING

We are cool.
Way cool.
Baseball cap, slung sideways,
cemented to hair
sheared ear to
here
left Rapunzel-like
on top.
Shoes—black—
fashionably loose-laced
and flopping, like
clumsy, odoriferous U-boats
gone AWOL on dry land.
Shirt, size XXL,
hawking in retro-neon
images Ricky and The Beav couldn't
conjure in their nastiest nightmare.
Pants, each leg approaching
dirigible girth,
billow ripped and wrinkled
against pale, hairless calves.
We are cool?
Well, we are fifteen.

FAMILY BUSINESS

Lesson in Economics #1:
if you save half your paycheck every week,
by the time you're twenty,
you'll be halfway to rich.
"So what do I have to do again?"
"Do I clock out if I go to the bathroom?"
*"Wow! In two months, I'll have over a
hundred dollars!"*

Lesson in Economics #2:
You cannot get paid for work you
do not do.
*"But Friday's my birthday! I don't have to work
on my birthday, do I?"*
*"I have a headache! You don't expect me to work
when I'm sick, do you?"*

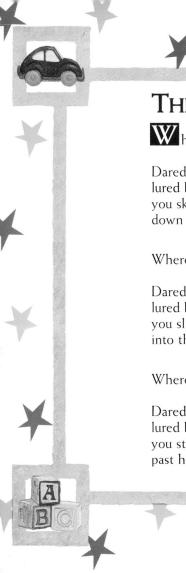

THE FUGITIVE

Where were you running, little one—
        toward, or away?
Dared by a dancing sunbeam,
lured by a languid frog,
you skipped off merrily
down the summer-dusty road
        toward adventure, away from mundane.

Where were you running, young man—
        toward, or away?
Dared by a taste of defiance,
lured by a laissez-faire lass,
you slipped out stealthily
into the fog-damp dawn
        toward a fantasy, away from the truth.

Where were you running, mister—
        toward, or away?
Dared by a vision of grandeur,
lured by lies you longed to believe,
you strolled on arrogantly
past hands and hearts stretched out to help
        toward tomorrow, away from today.

FAREWELL, MY DEAR ONE

You wouldn't like it,
I know,
but I've done it for
too many years.
So, taking advantage
of your slumbering senses,
I kiss your forehead, brush the hair
from your brow,
and whisper in your ear
the mantra that's been yours
since birth:
"I love you. I think you're wonderful.
I'm so glad that you're my son."
From those first nights when
I tiptoed in, holding my breath to listen
for yours,
through nights when you slept,
exhausted,

first from play, then from living,
then loving.
Now,
you lay here sprawled and tall—
a man's lean, hard body
below my little boy's soft, sweet face.
Tomorrow someone else will wake and kiss you
in the night.
Just this once, I bend and kiss you
twice.